Wolves In Sheep's Clothing

Jamie Lammers

BookLeaf Publishing

Presentation by *BookLeaf Publishing*

Web: www.bookleafpub.com

E-mail: info@bookleafpub.com

ISBN: 9789357612630

First edition 2022

DEDICATION

For Greg

PREFACE

"Thoughts are often wolves in sheep's clothing"

-A. Watts

Can We Talk?

If I have been silent
With you in my arms,
Then I have told you
Everything

On Vulnerability

Sometimes
When the Universe wants to open you up
It uses a man and goes through
your legs

Sweeps Week

3

Love is
A prize
You need
Not be
Present
To win

Heart Burn

Some people feel like
Eternity in a second-

Fast Food Love causes
Indigestion

Certain Death

You lay on top of me
Heavy and full
Like the dirt I imagine
Pressed onto my grave
And i wonder-
Why do I crave this?

Eros

6

I thanked God for you today
for stolen moments under the moon
and quiet glances full of fire

For soft, sweet kisses that make me feel like
a fine wine or piece of chocolate
you are considering devouring

Lost in Translation

7

Maybe I am
A language
You do not
speak

The Gambler

A heart is not
A coin
If you use it as such
Only you will end up
Spent

On Invisibility

The glue
Which binds
The world
Dries clear

Detachment

Happiness
Is a Nomad

Let her come,
Let her go

Whatever you do,
Don't hang on by your
Expectations

Adam's Rib

I am Adam's rib
You can't breathe right
Once you've got me fucked up

Babel

Be careful of their words, my friend
They are like your thoughts, often
Wolves
In sheep's clothing

YEWMEMBER

There is a poison
That creates a need
For antidote

Stop
Letting the damn snake
Bite you.

Muscle Memory

Now what?
Well.
Hearts are muscles
Muscles carry memory
She does not forget
Many moons may pass
Someday you will call on her
You will need her again
She will be ready
A strong muscle
With strong memory
Chambers Full

My Bad (On Self-Sabotage)

15

Trust.
(Open Your Eyes)
The word has two crosses
One for Him-
The other for You

LIFT

I'm going out into the world
to fly my heart like a kite

I hope I don't get the wind knocked out of her
this time

I watch her soar,
Led on by a string

I know she will soon strike
back down to hard Earth,

Hitting at a point that may collapse her
With its force

I know this
But still,
I fly the damn kite

Defensive Behavior

17

I feel Life
has backed me into a corner
and

It's all my fault
Somehow

Prayer from a Sleepless Night

Please God,
Don't shut the door on me
Just yet
Don't give up hope on me
So soon
I might be slower than
You'd like
But I'm still here looking
For you
Checking all the door and windows
Don't shut them yet
Please God,
Be like Motel 8 and
Leave a light on…

GRIMM

19

I am the knight
In shoddy armor,
And I will save
Myself

Strength

A repetition causes a microtear
In your tissue

And you see the damage
It's called a muscle

It happens this way
With spirit too

Occham's Razor

I carry a chip on my shoulder
I lose it from time to time
As my frazzled nerves grow older
Lost connections seem just fine

www.ingramcontent.com/pod-product-compliance
Lightning Source LLC
Chambersburg PA
CBHW070009250125
20806CB00047B/1177